THE
WONDROUS
WIZARD OF ID

Brant Parker and Johnny Hart

FAWCETT GOLD MEDAL • NEW YORK

A Fawcett Gold Medal Book

Published by Ballantine Books

ISBN 0-449-12619-6

This edition published by arrangement with Publishers-Hall
Syndicate, Inc.

Manufactured in the United States of America

First Fawcett Gold Medal Edition: August 1970
First Ballantine Books Edition: April 1983

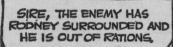

THE WIZARD REALLY FEELS BAD ABOUT THIS, RODNEY. HE IS WORKING ON THE ANTIDOTE FOR YOU.

HE WANTS TO KNOW HOW HE CAN MAKE YOU COMFORTABLE WHILE YOU ARE WAITING.

HE CAN GIVE SOME OF THAT POTION TO THESE CRUMMY PIGEONS.

IT'S NOT RIGHT, SIRE... WHY, THE CHAP IS **COMMERCIALIZING!**

HE'S TAKING ADVANTAGE OF HIS POSITION!... IT'S CONDUCT UNBECOMING AN OFFICER!

... BESIDES, HE'S GETTING **RICH!**

CALL SIR RODNEY.

YOU WANTED ME, SIRE?

EAT AT JOE'S

THE INITIAL TEST FOR KNIGHTHOOD IS SPEARTHROWING.

YOU MUST LEARN TO THROW A SPEAR 500 YARDS.

IT'S NOT EASY BEING AN EVIL SPIRIT, WITH SO MUCH COMPETITION ABOUT.

HOW LONG DID YOU SAY YOUR MOTHER IS STAYING?

THREE FULL MOONS.

POW

THE KING IS FURIOUS!...

WHY?

HIS FAVORITE TROUT STREAM IS FULL OF CURDS AND WHEY.

WHAT IS HE GOING TO DO?

HE ORDERED EVERY CHICKEN COOP IN THE KINGDOM BURNED DOWN.

THAT FIGURES... DURING THE EGG STRIKE HE DEHORNED ALL THE COWS.

SIRE, I FEAR THE CASTLE CRIER HAS GOTTEN WIND OF THE SPOOK'S *SWILL STRIKE.*

SO WHAT?

THEY MAY PRINT VICIOUS STORIES ABOUT DUNGEON CONDITIONS.

LET 'EM... MY DUNGEONS ARE OPEN TO ANYONE WHO WANTS TO TRY THEM!